Liverpool from the air

© The Bluecoat Press 1999

Published by The Bluecoat Press, Liverpool
Designed by March Design, Liverpool
Printed by Tenon & Polert

Front cover: Pier Head Liverpool 1960

ISBN 1 872568 45 9

Acknowledgements
My grateful thanks to the staff of the now defunct Liverpool City Engineer's
Reprographic Department who provided the 1930s aerial photographs and to
Liverpool Record Office for additional historical material. Also to Angela
Mounsey for her work in preparing the book for publication.

Liverpool from the air

Colin Wilkinson
with contemporary photographs by John Calderbank

The Bluecoat Press

Liverpool from the air

Top Lunardi's balloon demonstration in Liverpool.

Bottom Early photography from balloons was a precarious exercise. Vibrations apart, the photographs relied on a rapid descent to develop the glass plates while they were still wet.

The view of Earth from the air has transformed our way of seeing. From the earliest ascents in hot-air balloons, to breathtaking voyages into outer space, the aerial perspective has held a particular attraction. No other medium captures so accurately the history of our landscape at a particular time and, in Liverpool from the Air, two time periods – the 1930s and 1990s – are compared to show some of the effects of urban change during this century. The 1930s photographs were taken by the City Engineer's Department, flying out of the newly-opened Speke Airport. The 1990s photographs (taken between 1996-99) used the earlier photographs for reference in an attempt to duplicate the viewpoint as accurately as possible. The result is a fascinating comparison between the city of the 1930s, when a population of over 850,000 was squeezed into an area essentially contained within the boundary of Queens Drive and that of the 1990s, when the population of nearer 450,000 is spread over a substantially larger area.

Man's attempts to fly have been well-documented. Leonardo da Vinci was amongst many obsessed with the idea of man joining the birds although he appears to have concerned himself with the theoretical rather than the practical – unlike many inventors who hurtled to their deaths strapped to makeshift wings and machinery.

The first real breakthrough was by the Montgolfier brothers, whose pioneering experiments with hot air balloons resulted in the first public demonstration in 1783. Ballooning rapidly caught the public imagination and, by the following year, a Mr Lunardi was giving a public demonstration in Moorfields, in Liverpool, to a huge crowd of 150,000.

The new perspective gained from the balloon's basket was not lost on artists, who began to produce bird's eye views of townscapes. John Isaac's engraving of Liverpool is typical of the views that were commercially popular before the advent of aerial photography.

The invention of photography by Joseph Niepce in 1827, was a historical landmark, although it took his collaborator, Louis Jacques Daguerre, until 1838 to develop a practical method that had commercial implications. His daguerreotype, a unique, unduplicatable positive image fixed on a polished silver plate, was immediately in competition with a negative process invented by William Henry Fox Talbot, a wealthy English landowner and

scientist. However, the impact of photography was limited by its technology. Early processes required long exposures on plates that had to be prepared in situ and developed immediately after exposure. The balloon was a poor camera platform, it vibrated and, with several seconds required for exposures, a sharp exposure was almost impossible to achieve.

The first successful attempt, a murky view of Paris, was achieved by Nadar in 1858. A more impressive result was achieved by the American, James Wallace Black, who photographed Boston in 1860 from a height of 1200 feet. The process required, involved coating a glass plate with collodion silver nitrate and then exposing it whilst the collodion was still moist. Photographers had to be rapidly winched down in their balloons to make a quick dash for a mobile darkroom to develop the plates.

As the new technology of dry plates and hand cameras developed, aerial photography became as reliable as photography on the ground and its true potential could begin to be realised. Certain uses had already been considered, particularly military intelligence. German scientists had experimented with rockets from the 1890s onwards, firing a camera to an altitude of 2500 feet before the nose blew off and the camera descended on a parachute. A timing device triggered the exposure. More bizarre experiments included the use of pigeons, with cameras fastened to a harness around their bodies. The lightweight camera, weighing less than two ounces, took photographs automatically at thirty second intervals.

The twentieth century started with one of man's greatest technological breakthroughs. The first manned flight by the Wright Brothers in 1903 was a key moment in history, although it took time before the airplane became adaptable for photography. In fact, the first photographs from an airplane were taken by LP Bonvillain, a Pathé photographer, on a Wilbur Wright demonstration flight in France in 1908. (The first photographs from an airplane in England were taken in1910). The military was already aware of the advantages of aerial photography and the First World War proved the value of flying with a camera high above enemy lines.

Locally, the first significant date was 29 November 1910, when C Compton Patterson and RA King flew a bi-plane across the Mersey. Aeronautical progress was so rapid, that during the 1914-18 War,

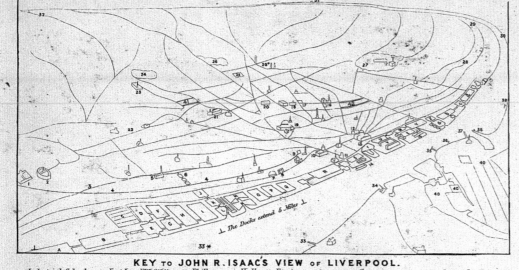

KEY TO JOHN R. ISAAC'S VIEW OF LIVERPOOL.

1 Industrial Schools	9 East Lanc.r R.y Station	16 Philharmonic Hall	22 Everton	29 Garston	34 Seacombe Ferry
2 Kirkdale Goal	10 Town Hall & Exchange	Church & Blind Asylum	23 West Derby Workhouse	30 Eastham	35 Woodside do
3 Canal	11 Tower Bldg.s & Telegraph	17 Medical Hall	24 Zoological Gardens	31 Runcorn	36 Monks do
4 East Lanc.r Railway	12 Sailors Home	18 Parish Buildings	25 Reservoir	32 S.t Helens	37 Birkenhead do
5 Cotton Mill	13 Custom House and	19 S.t Georges Hall - Church	26 Botanic Gardens	33 *Mouth of the River Mersey	38 Tranmere do
6 Canal Locks	Post Office	and L & N.W.R. Station	26 *Edge Hill R.y Station	41 Necropolis	39 Rock do
7 Borough Goal	14 Landing Stage & Baths	Infirmary	27 Princes Park	42 S.t James Cemetry	40 Birkenhead Docks,
8 Northern Hospital	15 Tobacco Warehouses	21 Collegiate Institution	28 Toxteth Park	33 Egremont Ferry	and Warehouses.

A Intended Dock	E Sanden Basin	I Nelson Dock	M Clarence Dock	Q Waterloo Dock	U Salthouse Dock	Y Queens Dock
B Huskisson do	F Wellington Dock	J Stanley do	N do.Half Tide Basin	R Princes do	V Albert do	Z Union do
C Sanden Graving Docks	G do. Half Tide Dock	K Collingwood do	O Trafalgar Dock	S Georges do	W Intended do	a Coburg do
D Sanden Dock	H Bramley-Moore do	L Salisbury do	P Victoria do	T Canning do	X Kings do	b Brunswick do
						c Toxteth do
						d Intended do

airplanes were being mass-manufactured in Liverpool.

The opening of Speke Airport in 1933 provided the opportunity to establish a world-class facility. It also created the impetus for the City Engineer to plot the city from the air and the fascinating photographs reproduced in this book are from a series of flights taken between 1933 and 1935. They show a densely-populated city with few green spaces. The Anglican Cathedral was still under construction and the workhouse on Brownlow Hill was in its last days before becoming the site of the Metropolitan Cathedral. The long line of the Overhead Railway can be seen running parallel with the river and the early demolition work for the first Mersey tunnel can be seen in Old Haymarket.

The comparative photographs provoke a host of questions about change in our city. The colour of the 1990s photographs certainly shows open space more clearly than the monochrome images of the 1930s but there is unquestionably less building density today. The endless rows of terraces have not vanished entirely but have been increasingly pushed back out of the city centre areas. The effect of bombing in the last war and comprehensive redevelopment, particularly in the 1960s, resulted in the major reshaping of many parts of the city. Changes in industry and commerce have made a major impact and huge factories which employed thousands, such as Tate and Lyle and British American Tobacco, have disappeared and their land has been taken by other developments. Warehouses, once the dominant feature of the city, have become almost a rarity and once-busy quaysides are now lined with luxury houses and docks transformed into tourist attractions. Each view reveals significant clues about our living standards and how Liverpool is shaping up to the twenty first century. Publishing these photographs will, hopefully, offer a valuable source of reference to anyone interested in urban change and add to our understanding of how Liverpool has developed as a city.

Left John Isaac's view of Liverpool was one of several attempts to capitalise commercially on the unique perspective gained from the balloon's basket.

Below The use of pigeons as aerial photographers must be one of the most bizarre examples of military intelligence gathering.

Right A German aerial photograph to be used to devastating effect in the Second World War.

Opposite Manufacturing RAF aircraft in Pleasant Street, Liverpool, 1918.

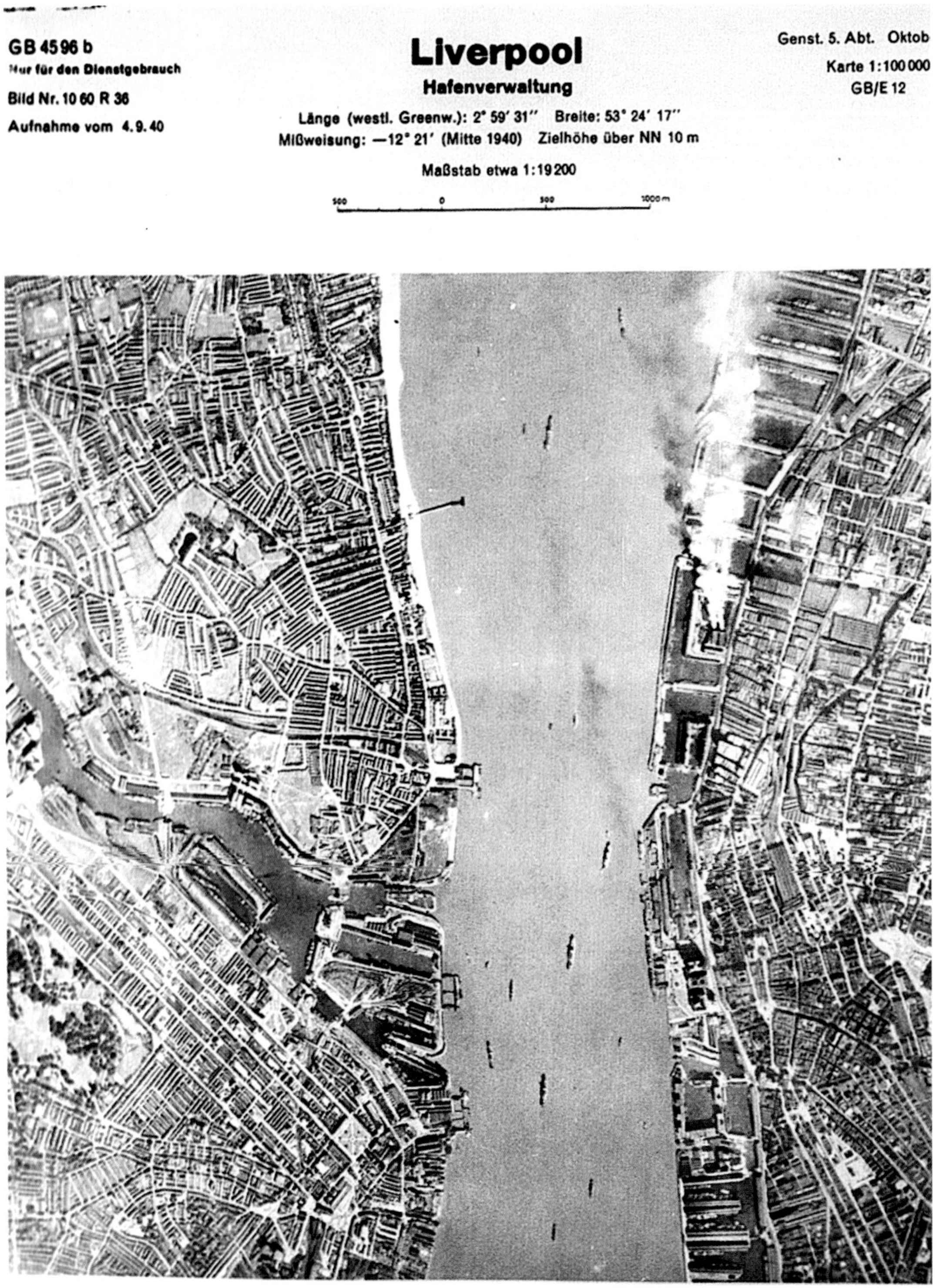

GB 45 96 b
Nur für den Dienstgebrauch

Bild Nr. 10 60 R 36

Aufnahme vom 4. 9. 40

Liverpool
Hafenverwaltung

Länge (westl. Greenw.): 2° 59′ 31″   Breite: 53° 24′ 17″
Mißweisung: —12° 21′ (Mitte 1940) Zielhöhe über NN 10 m

Maßstab etwa 1:19 200

500   0   500   1000 m

Genst. 5. Abt. Oktob

Karte 1:100 000
GB/E 12

Above A bi-plane flies above Wirral. Taken in 1910, the photograph is the earliest record of flight in this area.

Right The poster announcing the opening of Speke Airport.

Opposite Lost Liverpool. Three major post-War developments had significant effects for existing building stock.

Top Left The Custom House site in the process of being cleared.

Top right The destruction of St John's Market and the surrounding network of streets to make way for the new market.

Bottom Left The removal of rows of terraced housing to create the site of the Royal Liverpool Hospital.

Bottom right In the 1970s, a huge swathe of land was cut through the Scotland Road area to create access to the Kingsway Tunnel.

Garston

The two views show remarkably little change at first glance. The key feature, the dock, which opened in 1846, has lost its warehousing and railway yard but is still economically active. The predominance of heavy industry (including a tannery and copper works) has been reduced and landscaping has replaced cleared sites. Garston Gas Works opened in 1881 and closed in 1969, and the two gasometers are still a towering feature. Garston has retained much of its village character and the dense area of terraced housing has remained surprisingly intact.

Aigburth

The Victorian private housing estates of Cressington Park and Grassendale Park are in the immediate foreground and show only minor changes from the 1930s. Post-war housing development has increasingly encroached on the area, nibbling away at the edges but the green space has held remarkably well. The key change has been the construction of Otterspool Promenade, a massive engineering project which started in the 1930s, as can be seen in the earlier photograph. Using rubble from the excavations of the Mersey Tunnel, amongst other sources, a superb riverside parkland was developed within the new river defenses. Dingle Point and jetty (the 'Cast Iron Shore') and oil storage tanks can be seen top centre of the 1930s view. The International Garden Festival of 1984 reclaimed the land for recreational and private housing use and the riverside walk has been extended.

Toxteth Dock and Dingle

Toxteth Dock opened in 1888 and was serviced by the Brunswick Goods Yard with its extensive rail network. Light industrial units now fill the converted warehouses in what has been a successful attempt to revitalise the redundant dock areas. In the 1930s photograph, the line of Liverpool Overhead Railway can be seen running parallel to Sefton Street with Brunswick Station left centre. The line of the Overhead can be seen (top right) running over the cantilever bridge, before entering a tunnel to take it to Dingle Station. Above the goods yard, on Caryl Street, the chimney and remains of the Mersey Forge are forlorn reminders of a once-important industry. The gasometer, left centre, is still a dominant feature, dwarfing Beaufort Street Board School. The school has just closed down, after serving the community for over a century, to merge with nearby Park Hill School on a new site. Just behind the gasometer, the remains of the old mill, without its sails, can still be seen. The mill, built before 1820, survived until the 1960s. Flour milling still continues on the site – a rare continuity in an area where so much has changed. The modern view shows new low-density housing gradually replacing the closely-packed terraces.

Wapping Warehouse

Wapping Warehouse, designed by Jesse Hartley, opened in 1856. Its commercial life was over by the 1970s and the building stood empty until it was converted into luxury flats in the early 1990s. The original warehouse was a bay longer until the blitz but the original length was not reinstated (although the cast-iron columns have been retained as a feature). Wapping Station on the Overhead Railway can be clearly seen to the immediate right of the warehouse. Across the road, the change is more marked. The huge goods warehouse of the LMS Railway runs from Wapping to Park Lane. Fed by an underground railway tunnel to Crown Street, the depot was an important link in the transport network. The depot has since been demolished, although the office building remains in Park Lane. The future of the tunnel has recently been raised as a possible road link into the city centre.

Warehousing was once the most dominant feature along the length of the Dock Road but modern businesses require ground floor storage for forklift operations – not multi-storey bays with access by hoist. There is a limit to the number of alternative uses and most of the warehouses have ben demolished. The yellow building with a blue roof, just behind the Wapping Warehouse, is the new YHA hostel, another sign of Liverpool's burgeoning tourist trade.

Albert Dock

The Albert Dock was opened by Prince Albert in 1846. Now a major tourist attraction, the Dock warehouses were the first fully-enclosed system built within Liverpool Docks. Commercially, the dock was not a great success, its entrance proving too small for a new generation of merchant steamships. Fortunately, somewhat against the odds, the monumental structure has been conserved and now houses museums, galleries, retail units, luxury flats and offices. Sadly, its neighbour, Dukes Dock Warehouses (on the right corner of Albert Dock) was demolished in the 1960s to make way for, as it proved, short-lived storage sheds. Now, that whole area has been cleared and is currently used for car parking, although plans for a major development are anticipated. The Custom House is discernible with its prominent dome. Fire-bombed in the war, it was salvageable but the decision to demolish it deprived the city of one of its finest buildings. Its replacement, the concrete and glass Canning Place, can be seen shrouded in green netting during demolition.

Pier Head

The Pier Head is the city's most impressive display of confidence; an unmistakable group of buildings famous throughout the world. Changes have taken place: the Overhead Railway has gone, as have the Goree Warehouses which can be seen running alongside it. The Port of Liverpool, Cunard and Royal Liver Buildings stand unchanged, apart from relatively recent stone-cleaning, as symbols of the city's prosperity in the early twentieth century. The Port of Liverpool Building with its Classical dome, headquarters of the Mersey Docks and Harbour Board, was completed in 1908. The Corporation had intended a similar building to be built on the adjacent site to give symmetry to the waterfront. Fortunately, the Royal Liver Friendly Society had other ideas and had the inspiration to employ Walter A Thomas as architect. His Royal Liver Building, completed in 1911, is unforgettable, one of the great English buildings of this century. The Cunard, sandwiched in between its flamboyant neighbours, was the last to be completed, in 1916. The 1990s photograph shows recent landscaping to the frontage. The bus terminus has been replaced by an attractive grassed and paved public area, although the ferry terminal and restaurant are hardly fitting buildings for such a prestigious site.

Prince's Dock

In the foreground of the 1990s photograph, the redevelopment of Prince's Dock is rapidly taking shape with accountants' offices facing the river and the Crown Plaza Hotel on the other side of the partly filled-in dock. The dock, which opened in 1821, was active until the 1960s. Its future is now for mixed commercial use that will bring new life to an area which has lain derelict for decades.

Beyond the Dock Road, change is equally dramatic. The dominant feature in the 1930s, was the concentration of warehouses. Work on the entry to the Queensway Tunnel can be seen in the bottom right of the photograph. The long roof of Exchange Station almost dwarfs the remains of St Paul's Church, which is in the final stages of demolition. To the right are the flamboyant towers of the Cotton Exchange (completed in 1906), which were removed in the 1960s to be replaced by a less distinguished facade. In the surrounding area, fitting in around the offices and factories, are streets of congested slum housing, amongst the worst in the city.

Canada Dock

Canada Dock opened as a timber dock in 1858. The hand of Jesse Hartley can be seen in the 1930s view. His octagonal hydraulic gate-house was one of his most remarkable creations with its castellated tower. Sadly, as the 1990s photograph clearly shows, the reworking of the entrance to the dock removed the need for the lock. Perhaps the major change has been the removal of most of the sheds, the cleared areas now being used largely for scrap metal storage. Outside the dock walls, the heavy concentration of warehousing and heavy industry has been considerably reduced to make way for light industrial and business units.

Parliament Street and Park Lane

The 1990s view shows a wider perspective, taking in Cain's Brewery and Parliament Street in the foreground. Facing the brewery are the huge warehouses on the corner of Jamaica Street. Warehouses on this scale were once commonplace the length of the dock network. Today, there is little call for vertical storage space. Hopefully, this impressive example will be preserved as an essential piece of the city's heritage.

This is the area written about by Pat O'Mara in his *Autobiography of a Liverpool Slummy*. The slum housing he describes so vividly can be seen in the shadow of the Wapping Station Goods Warehouse. Someone has given token recognition to the needs of children: in the foreground is a playground on the corner of Norfolk Street. Otherwise, the only open space is St George's Square (top right) and the grounds of St Michael's Church in Pitt Street (the church, one of the finest in Liverpool, was bombed in 1941 and subsequently demolished). The 1990s view reflects changes that have transformed much of the city. The slums have been removed and the population density of the area has been dramatically reduced. In the last ten years, new housing has been built along the length of Park Lane and, slowly, the area's decline is being addressed with new business units and general environmental improvements.

Liverpool Cathedral

The building of Liverpool Cathedral started in 1906 and, by the mid-1930s, work on the tower was about to start. Housing runs down the hill, with the open space of Great George's Square (bottom left) once boasting some of the city's finest housing. By 1930, the square had lost its status and was at the centre of an extensive triangle of slums running from Great George Street down Duke Street and along Park Lane and St James Street. The housing fronting the Cathedral was finally removed by the late 1970s including, (bottom right) the David Lewis Hostel and Theatre, on the corner of Great George Street and Parliament Street. A proposal to landscape the cleared area as a public park was rejected in favour of a scheme to bring people back into the area. The move to build new housing in such areas, rather than on greenfield sites in the suburbs, is proving successful in regenerating the inner-city.

Upper Parliament Street and Prince's Road

The uniformity of the terraces is a striking feature of the 1930s photograph. The rows of Victorian houses were a step-up from the slums of nearby Park Lane and, in the 1930s, the area was regarded as a good residential area. After the War, the housing stock deteriorated and most of the terraces have now disappeared, although many of the mansions lining Prince's Road have survived. The road connected Prince's Park with the town and, following the completion of the park in 1846, there was a rush of speculative building to cater for Liverpool's growing middle-class. An impressive feature of the area is the number of fine church buildings. The Greek Orthodox Church of St Nikolas (1870) catered for Liverpool's large Greek community, whilst on the other side of the road, the magnificent synagogue (1874) was a symbol of the confidence of the well-established Jewish community. Next door, the Church of St Margaret (1869) boasts a fine interior and, along the road, the spire of the Presbyterian Church of Wales is one of the areas most recognisable features. Fortunately, all four churches survive, if somewhat precariously, although the Rialto Ballroom, which faces the Orthodox Church in the 1930s photograph, was burnt down in the 1981 Toxteth Riots. The 1990s photograph shows a cleared site which has since been built on.

City Centre

The line of Hanover Street runs through the centre of the photograph. Street after street of warehouses dominate the foreground. The impressive facades of Lord Street and Church Street can be seen running diagonally from the bottom right corner. The central area was badly-affected by bombing during the war and reconstruction was inevitable. However, the extent of redevelopment has been a long-running source of public indignation. A number of key architectural losses to the city are evident, particularly St John's Market, the Theatre Royal in Williamson Square and the splendid cast-iron vaulting of Central Station (mid-right). Perhaps as great a loss has been the destruction of the pattern of small streets and squares with their fascinating mix of merchant houses, pubs, warehouses and offices. The rush for modernisation in the post-war years replaced character with uniformity, stone and bricks with concrete. The symbol of those philistine years, St John's Beacon, a concrete white elephant is the dominant feature of the 1990s photograph whilst, in the foreground, the demolition of the ugly 1970s Canning Place complex is an apt statement on architectural brutalism.

St George's Hall

The key feature in the foreground is the commencement of work on the first Mersey Tunnel. The facades of Old Haymarket are being cleared to make way for one of the great engineering achievements of the inter-war years. Beyond are the long roofs of St John's Market (opened in 1822) and the surrounding market area. Interestingly, there is very little traffic or evidence of market activity. Queen Square, on the Haymarket side of St John's Market, is empty of carts and people, suggesting the photograph was taken on a Sunday. Noticeable in all the older photographs is the effect of years of smoke damage to the buildings. The blackened facades of St George's Hall and, behind, the North Western Hotel, hide the beauty of the stonework which is so evident in the 1990s photograph. To many people, Victorian architecture conjured up a grim and dour image, which cleaning has done much to dispel. Perhaps more of the city's buildings would have been saved had their visual qualities not been lost behind decades of soot and grime. In the 1990s photograph, the latest wave of redevelopment can be seen with the completion of the new Queen Square development on the fringe of St John's Garden.

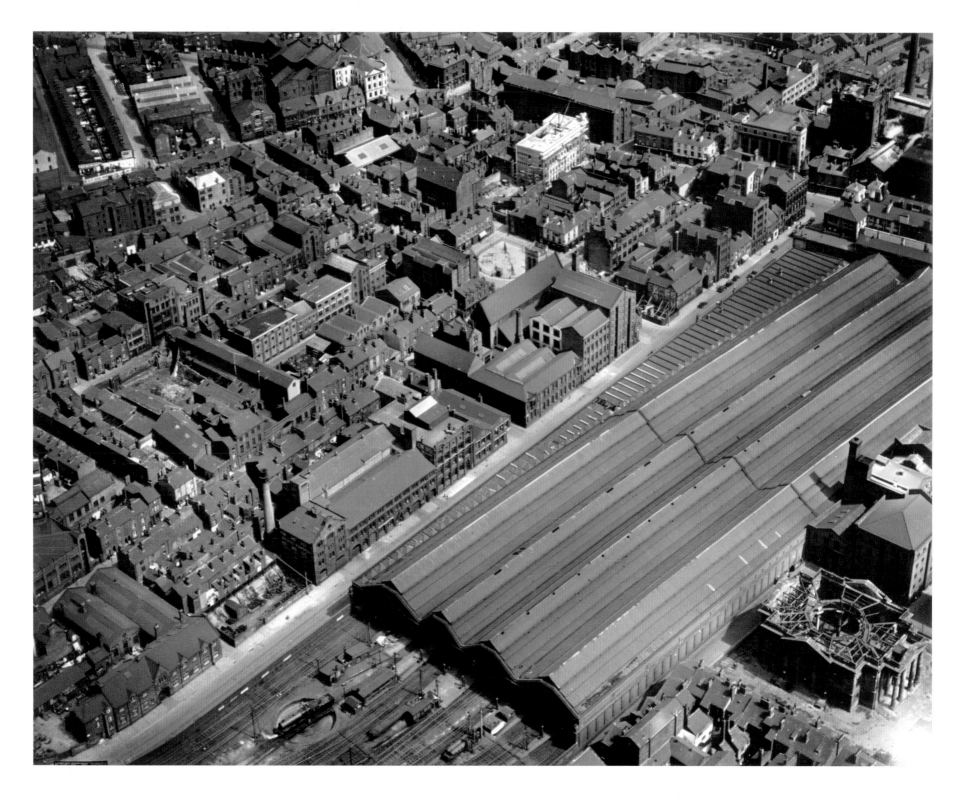

Exchange Station

Exchange Station dominates the photograph. Opened in 1850, it was rebuilt and renamed Liverpool Exchange in 1888. The main railway to Southport, it closed in 1977 and faced an uncertain future. Fortunately, the station facade to Tithebarn Street was retained, although the platform areas made way for an office development. In the right hand corner, the camera has captured the demolition of St Paul's Church. Built in 1769, the church was a combination of St Paul's Cathedral and St Stephen's, Walbrook, in London. Much admired, the church was cleared along with much of the slum housing in the area. On the other side of Pall Mall, a similar level of slum clearance was about to take place with modern tenements built along Fontenoy Street and Leeds Street. The 1990s photograph shows vestiges of older buildings along Pall Mall but most of these have since been cleared to make way for new housing. The 1960s block in the foreground is the JM Centre, headquarters of the Littlewood Group.

Metropolitan Cathedral of Christ the King

A rare and fascinating view of Liverpool Workhouse. A town within a town, the high walls concealed 150 years of human misery. Opened in 1771, the population rapidly expanded until, by 1910, there were 5000 occupants crammed into overcrowded wards where men were separated from women, as families were split up to preserve an obsolete and, by today's standards, obscene Victorian morality. In 1930, the land was sold to the Catholic Church as the site for a new cathedral. The original cathedral, a masterpiece of huge proportions, was designed by Sir Edwin Lutyens and the foundations and crypt were constructed before the outset of the Second World War. The war, and deaths of both Lutyens and Archbishop Downey, robbed the building of its momentum and, in the changed climate of the post-war years, a different, cheaper solution was sought. The result was the splendid 'wigwam' designed by Frederick Gibberd and now a well-loved feature on the skyline. To the east of the cathedral, the lines of early Victorian terracing were pulled down to make way for the expansion of the University of Liverpool.

The University of Liverpool and Royal Infirmary

The circular wards of the Royal Infirmary stand out. Designed by Alfred Waterhouse, in consultation with Florence Nightingale, the hospital was opened in 1890 and represented a major step forward in medical care. By the 1950s, the hospital was deemed unsuitable for the changes in surgical and medical provision and a new hospital was proposed. The 1990s photograph shows the impact this new facility has had on a previously highly-populated area. The university also expanded outward, clearing the area of housing beyond the Royal Infirmary. Two other features stand out; the deep railway cuttings on the right and the semi-circular tenement block of St Andrew's Gardens. Locally known as the Bullring, the flats have been recently converted to student accommodation.

West Derby Road

The 1930s photograph is dominated by Ogden's Tobacco Factory, opened in 1899. Tobacco was one of the city's largest industries and Liverpool once boasted the largest warehouse in the world, at Stanley Dock, solely to store imported tobacco leaf. Ogden's still functions, although the other factories have closed down as changes in technology have led to a drastic rationalisation of the industry. In the bottom left hand corner is Mill Road Hospital. The density of housing has also been thinned out, with welcome green spaces appearing around modern housing estates.

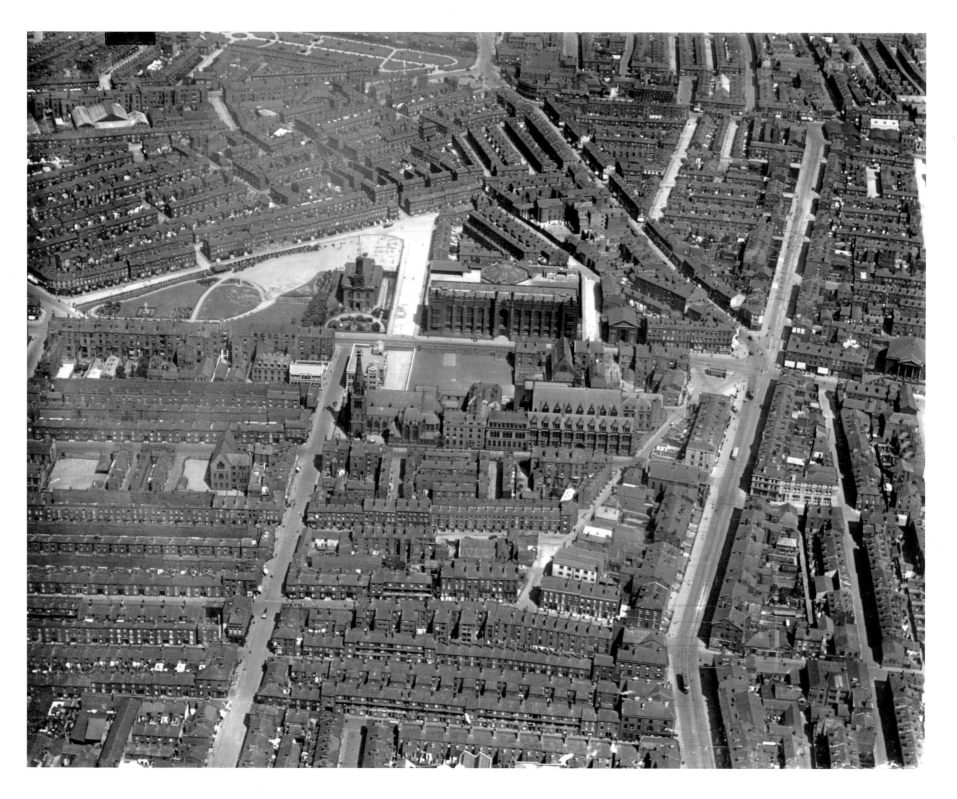

Islington and Shaw Street

Shaw Street was once one of Liverpool's most desirable addresses; so desirable that the Collegiate Institution, the forerunner of a new wave of public schools, was built in 1843 to the design of Harvey Elmes, the architect of St George's Hall. The gothic facade of the Collegiate can be seen mid-top to the right of the triangular plot of open space. Empty for years and badly-damaged by fire, the Collegiate is being converted into flats. Immediately in front is St Xavier's Church and School. In the 1990s photograph, the area to the left of the Collegiate is being landscaped into a new city park. New housing is regenerating the area and, to the right, following the line of Islington, modern warehousing and small business units have replaced dense housing. In the distance, the three tower blocks of Sheil Park stand out.

St Anne's Street

St Anne's Street runs left to right along the foreground of the photograph. Originally laid out in the late-eighteenth century, with impressive mansions for wealthy merchants, the street housed the travelling circuit judges until 1868, when a new house was built in Newsham Park. The church, bottom left, is St Anne's Church, consecrated in 1772, which marked the end of St Anne's Street and the start of Cazneau Street. Richmond Row runs diagonally up the hill from right to left.

This was an area of desperate slums. As the town expanded, the merchants were forced to leave for safer areas as the tenements rapidly encroached. Not a blade of grass is visible. A miserable triangular patch has been laid out as a playground off Christian Street (right foreground) and there is an open-air swimming bath on Birkett Street to the right of Richmond Row. Otherwise, the scene is one of unrelieved poverty.

The area has been cleared of most of its Victorian legacy. Some old housing survives on Fox Street, off Richmond Row, but the slums have been replaced by a mix of new housing and small business units. The modern building in the foreground on St Anne's Street is a police headquarters. Everton Park can be seen taking shape on the north end of Richmond Row.

Vauxhall Road

In the bottom left corner of the 1930s photograph, canal boats loaded with coal are lined up alongside the Leeds Liverpool Canal, waiting to discharge their cargo at the gas works. The canal is dominated by heavy industry. Cheap labour was never a problem, with one of the city's heaviest concentrations of slum property on the doorstep. A children's playground on Athol Street breaks up the monotony of the rows of terraces, with their infamous court housing.

Liverpool's population has declined considerably since the 1931 Census recorded a population of 852,000. By 1961, the total had fallen to 745,710 with a sharp drop to 698,834 in 1971. The downward trend has continued: to 509,834 in 1981 and 480,749 in 1991 (the last Census). The reduction in population and the collapse of industry in the area has created the opportunity to landscape the canal environment. Inspired by the example of the Eldonian Co-operative, new housing has been constructed and the community has been kept together.

The large, red-brick factory on the bank of the canal belonged to the British American Tobacco Company. A major employer in the area, it was an early victim of the economic recession of the 1980s.

Litherland Road and Marsh Lane

Superficially, the two photographs show surprisingly little change. The rows of terraced housing on the right have largely disappeared and the extent of the gas works reduced but much of the housing stock remains, as well as the land allocated to industry. The Leeds Liverpool Canal runs through the area and recent landscaping can be seen along its banks.

Hornby Boulevard and Linacre Road

The shape of the area has been determined by the sweep of the railway embankment. The large factory in the centre of the 1930s photograph is the Diamond Match Works, built in 1895. The company amalgamated with Bryant and May in 1901 and the factory survived until 1941, when it was damaged in an air raid. After the war, the business was moved to Garston and the factory site made over to housing.

The land beyond the top of the photograph was open countryside in the 1930s but, as the later view clearly shows, the green fields have been built on to accommodate the urban sprawl.

Walton Vale

The Black Bull public house stands at the junction of Longmoor Lane and Warbreck Moor and the Cheshire Lines Railway, now disused, runs under Walton Vale. The land to the right of Longmoor Lane has been given over to housing but, elsewhere, much of the area remains relatively unchanged.

Norris Green

As far back as 1869, Liverpool began a programme of slum clearance. Between 1869 and 1912, 12,000 insanitary buildings were demolished and 2,895 tenements erected. The tenements were vastly superior to the dreadful properties they had replaced but the housing programme could not keep pace with a steadily-increasing population and the inevitable deterioration of the housing stock.

The ending of the 1914-18 War gave an added urgency to provide better housing and the inspired leadership of Lancelot Keay, Liverpool's Director of Housing, resulted in a switch to cottage-type housing, built on the fringes of Queen's Drive, the new orbital roadway.

Norris Green was a large country house and grounds, and its purchase by the City led to the building of the large estate, laid out with geometrical precision between Utting Avenue and Muirhead Avenue.

The estate has kept its shape but beyond Dwerryhouse Lane, the rural aspect has been transformed by new housing.

West Derby

Alder Hey Children's Hospital is located at the bottom left corner, with Eaton Road running alongside it. The centre of West Derby village is towards the top of the photograph and the long driveway to Croxteth Hall can be seen running through open land.

Building work on the corner of Honey's Green Lane and Leyfield Road is in progress in the 1930s photograph and further building has since absorbed more agricultural land to the right.

Had the photograph been taken a few years earlier, the whole area would have been covered with fields. The ancient village of West Derby was one of the oldest in SW Lancashire and, at one time, was more important than Liverpool. The balance of power had long-since changed and the rural life had, by the early 1930s been overwhelmed by the encroachment of the city.

Hunts Cross

Another case of town meeting country. In the left corner is Allerton Cemetery with the railway running alongside. The green fields to the right are now a large retail complex, dominated by Asda Stores. To the right of the 1930s photograph, Speke Boulevard is in the process of being constructed, linking the new 'township' of Speke with Liverpool. The Speke Estate was purchased by the Liverpool Council in 1929 and 341 acres were set aside for industry, to be later extended by a further 100 acres.

Speke was planned as a self-contained township, with a targeted population of 25,000. War delayed its completion but, by 1954, all the housing had been completed. Unfortunately, many of the planned social provisions failed to materialise, leaving the area somewhat isolated.

The build-up of industry rapidly followed the road extension and the 1990s photograph shows the extent of industrialisation from the Ford Motor Company (top right), which opened in 1962, to the factory units lining the Liverpool to London rail link. The expansion of Halewood out towards Widnes seems to suggest that an aerial photograph, taken sixty years in the future, would show the fields presently separating the two having disappeared beneath bricks and concrete.

Goodison Park

Home of Everton Football Club, Goodison Park opened on 24 August, 1892. The record attendance of the old ground was a remarkable 78,299, although safety standards were considerably less stringent than today. The capacity of the ground is now 40,260. Goodison Park was one of the grounds chosen for the 1966 World Cup, hosting all of Brazil's matches, and was the competition's main venue outside Wembley

Everton has won the League Championship nine times, the Division 2 Championship once, the FA Cup five times and the European Cup Winners' Cup once, in 1985.

Anfield

Anfield, home of Liverpool Football Club, opened on 28 September, 1884. The record attendance for the old ground was 61,905 but safety standards at today's all-seater ground, have reduced the capacity to 45,362. Anfield was the site of the first Match of the Day broadcast on 22 August, 1964 and was chosen as one of the venues for the 1996 European Championship.

Liverpool FC have the best club record in England, having won the Championship on no fewer than eighteen occasions. Four Division 2 titles, five FA Cups, five League Cups, two UEFA Cups and four European Cups have filled the shelves of the club's impressive trophy room.

A final statement on the changes that have taken place over sixty years. The South Docks may have lost its commercial shipping but new uses to the vacated land have been found. The new marina is rapidly expanding and private housing now lines the quaysides. The yellow building in mid-shot is the new HM Customs and Excise building and, in the distance, the Albert Dock is now the city's major tourist attraction. There is still room for development, King's Dock, in front of the Albert Dock, is an obvious prime site and, no doubt the cleared area will add to the mix of offices, tourist and leisure attractions and housing that is creating an exciting future for Liverpool.